WHAT'S UNDER THE SEA?

Sophy Tahta

Designed by Sharon Bennet

Illustrated by Stuart Trotter

Consultant: Sheila Anderson

CONTENTS

Under the sea

Under the sea lies an amazing world of strange sea creatures, coral reefs, hidden wrecks and buried pipelines.

Different things go on in different parts of the sea, from the surface down to the seabed.

The surface is lit by the sun. Most plants and animals live here.

People explore the sea in special diving suits and underwater machines.

The deepest part of the sea is cold and dark. It is called the abyss.

Weird-looking fish and other animals live in the deep sea and on the seabed below.

The deep seabed is covered with wide plains, high mountains and deep trenches.

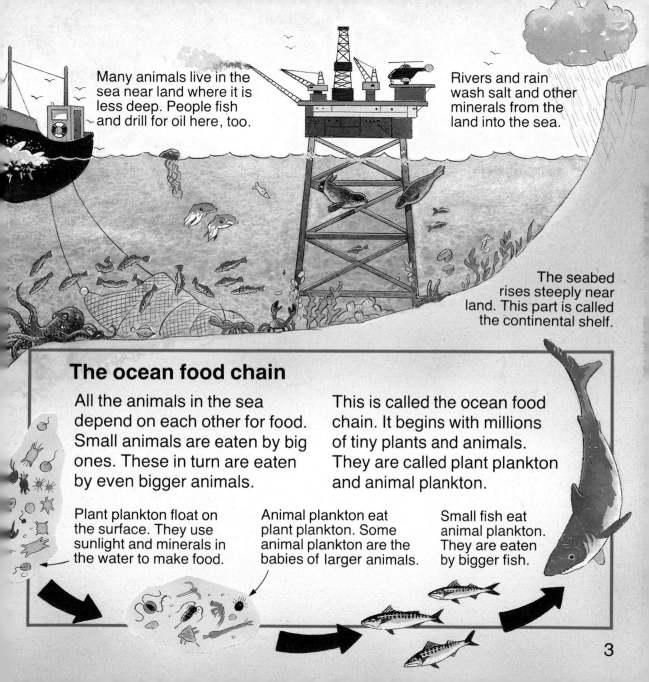

Many animals live in the sea near land where it is less deep. People fish and drill for oil here, too.

Rivers and rain wash salt and other minerals from the land into the sea.

The seabed rises steeply near land. This part is called the continental shelf.

The ocean food chain

All the animals in the sea depend on each other for food. Small animals are eaten by big ones. These in turn are eaten by even bigger animals.

This is called the ocean food chain. It begins with millions of tiny plants and animals. They are called plant plankton and animal plankton.

Plant plankton float on the surface. They use sunlight and minerals in the water to make food.

Animal plankton eat plant plankton. Some animal plankton are the babies of larger animals.

Small fish eat animal plankton. They are eaten by bigger fish.

3

Seas of the world

Over two-thirds of the Earth's surface is covered by sea. Different parts have different names and the largest areas are called oceans. All of the world's seas and oceans are linked together.

The warmest seas lie near the Equator, an imaginary line around the middle of the Earth.

The coldest seas lie near the North and South Poles, far away from the Equator.

North Pole
Equator

Pacific Ocean
South Pole

Currents

Water moves around the oceans in underwater rivers called currents. Warm currents flow near the surface but cold ones flow deeper down. This is because cold water is heavier than warm water.

The tallest mountain on Earth is Mauna Kea which forms the island of Hawaii. It rises 10,203m (33,476ft) from its base on the seabed.

Canada

USA

Atlantic Ocean

Hawaii

Equator

The world's largest mountain ridge runs under the Atlantic Ocean.

Red arrows show warm currents. They carry warm water from the Equator to cooler places.

The largest ocean is the Pacific Ocean. It covers about one third of the world.

South America

Blue arrows show cold currents. They carry cold water from the Poles to warmer places.

4

Arctic Ocean

The smallest ocean is the frozen Arctic Ocean.

Russia

The Persian Gulf is the warmest sea in the world.

Europe

The Marianas Trench is the deepest part of the sea.

Middle East

There are many coral islands in the Pacific Ocean.

The Red Sea is the saltiest sea in the world.

India

China

Pacific Ocean

Africa

Indian Ocean

Australia

The Great Barrier Reef is the world's biggest coral reef.

The biggest icebergs float in the Southern Ocean.

Southern Ocean

5

What is a fish?

Over 20,000 kinds of fish live in the sea. Fish are scaly animals with fins. They are also cold-blooded. This means that their bodies are always the same temperature as the sea.

Keeping afloat

Most fish have a bag of air like a small, thin balloon inside them. This is called a swim bladder. It helps them to stay afloat in the water without having to swim.

How do fish breathe?

Fish need oxygen to live. They cannot breathe it through the air, but water also has oxygen in it. Fish have special parts called gills which take oxygen from the water.

A fish beats its tail from side to side to push itself forward.

Fins help steer and balance the fish.

Slimy scales help fish glide through water.

Lateral line

Water goes in the mouth, over the gills and out of the gill covers above. Blood in the gills takes in oxygen.

A sixth sense

Most fish have a line along each side called a lateral line. This helps them to sense the movements that other animals make in the water.

Gill cover

6

Deep-sea fish

Some of the strangest fish live in the deep sea where it is dark and cold. They have special ways of finding food.

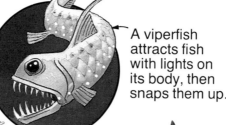

A viperfish attracts fish with lights on its body, then snaps them up.

An angler fish has a light on its head. Fish swim up to it and are gobbled up.

Hatchet fish have huge, bulging eyes that point up looking for food.

A gulper eel gulps down fish with its gaping mouth and long, stretchy belly.

Sharks and rays

Sharks and rays are among the biggest fish in the sea. They do not have swim bladders so they must keep swimming or they will sink.

Sharks have rows of razor-sharp teeth. When the front ones wear down, back ones move forward to take their place.

Great white shark

The manta ray flaps its side fins to swim. It leaps out of the water to escape danger.

Whales

Whales are the largest animals in the sea. They are not fish, but mammals. Mammals breathe air. They are also warm-blooded. This means that their bodies stay warm even when the sea is cold.

Baleen whales gulp in water and krill, then sift the water out through their baleen.

Baleen

Baleen whales

Some whales, such as humpback whales, do not have teeth. They have fringes of bristle called baleen instead. These whales eat tiny shrimps called krill.

Blow-hole

A whale comes to the surface to breathe air through a blow-hole on its head.

Krill

Whales have lots of fat, called blubber, to keep them warm.

Whales in danger

So many big whales have been hunted that there are far fewer left. Most countries have stopped hunting them, but a few still do.

Humpback whale

Whales with teeth

Other whales, such as sperm whales, have sharp teeth to eat fish, squid and other animals. They find food by making clicking noises.

These clicks bounce off animals in their way and send back echoes. The whale listens to the echoes to find out where the animal is.

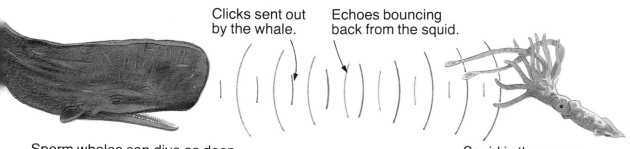

Clicks sent out by the whale.

Echoes bouncing back from the squid.

Sperm whales can dive as deep as 3,000m (9,000ft).

Squid is the sperm whale's main food.

Whale sizes

Whales come in all sizes. The smallest ones are porpoises and dolphins and the biggest ones are blue whales. Blue whales are the largest animals in the world.

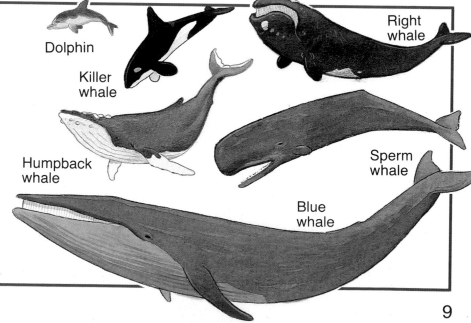

Dolphin

Killer whale

Right whale

Humpback whale

Sperm whale

Blue whale

9

Coral Reefs

Coral reefs are like beautiful underwater gardens. They grow in warm, shallow seas and are home to all sorts of fish and other animals.

What are corals?

Corals come in all shapes and sizes. They are built up from the stony skeletons of tiny animals called coral polyps. Polyps live on the surface of corals. When they die, new polyps grow on top.

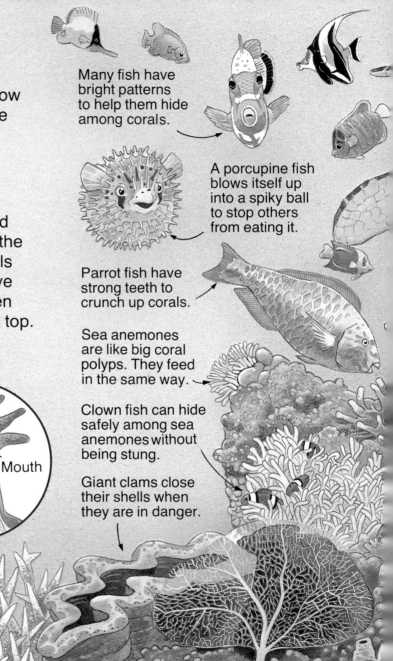

This is a close-up of a coral polyp cut in half. It uses its tentacles to sting animal plankton and put them in its mouth.

Tentacle   Mouth

Skeleton

Most coral polyps hide in their cup-shaped skeletons during the day. They come out to feed at night.

Corals build up into giant reefs over thousands of years.

Many fish have bright patterns to help them hide among corals.

A porcupine fish blows itself up into a spiky ball to stop others from eating it.

Parrot fish have strong teeth to crunch up corals.

Sea anemones are like big coral polyps. They feed in the same way.

Clown fish can hide safely among sea anemones without being stung.

Giant clams close their shells when they are in danger.

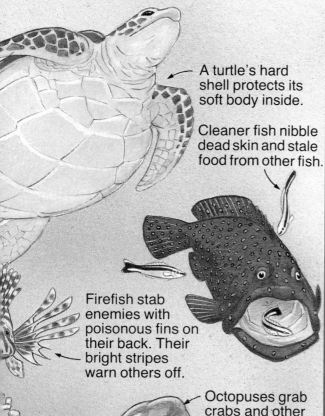

A turtle's hard shell protects its soft body inside.

Cleaner fish nibble dead skin and stale food from other fish.

Firefish stab enemies with poisonous fins on their back. Their bright stripes warn others off.

Octopuses grab crabs and other animals with their long tentacles.

Crown-of-thorns starfish feed on corals. They are destroying many reefs.

Coral islands

Coral islands often start as a fringe of coral which grows around the tip of an undersea volcano.

Side view

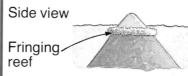

Fringing reef

The tip of the volcano forms an island.

The seabed slowly sinks taking the volcano down with it. The coral grows up to form a barrier reef.

Top view

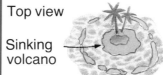

Sinking volcano

Barrier reefs grow offshore.

The sunken volcano leaves behind a ring of coral islands called an atoll. The sea inside is called a lagoon.

Top view

Lagoon

Coral atolls have no island inside.

Reefs under threat

Many reefs are damaged by people collecting coral and by pollution. A few are now protected as sea parks.

11

Icy seas

The coldest seas lie near the North and South Poles. They are called polar seas. They freeze over in autumn and melt in spring. Even so, many animals live in and around them.

Chunks of ice called icebergs float in polar seas. Some break off from rivers of ice called glaciers which slide off the land. Others break off from shelves of ice which stick out from the land.

As they melt, icebergs break up into smaller chunks called bergy bits.

Icebergs slowly drift into warmer water where they melt.

Most of an iceberg lies underwater. Only the tip shows above.

Penguins

Penguins are sea birds which cannot fly. They use their wings as flippers to swim underwater. Most penguins live in the southern polar seas.

Penguins can swim fast through the water. They leap out of the water to breathe air.

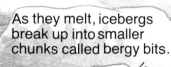

Penguins have a thick layer of fat, called blubber, and waterproof feathers to keep them warm.

Krill

Swarms of krill live in polar seas. Most polar animals eat krill, including whales which feed in polar seas in summer.

Penguins dive down for fish, krill and squid.

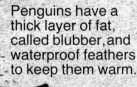

12

Seals

Seals are mammals which live mostly underwater. They come up to the surface to breathe air. Many seals live in the cold polar seas.

In winter, ringed seals scrape holes in the ice to breathe through.

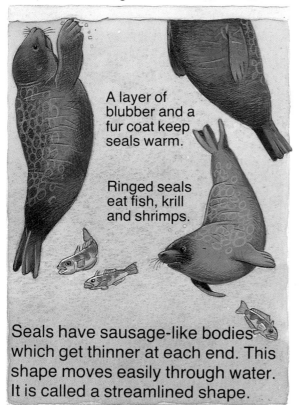

A layer of blubber and a fur coat keep seals warm.

Ringed seals eat fish, krill and shrimps.

Seals have sausage-like bodies which get thinner at each end. This shape moves easily through water. It is called a streamlined shape.

Polar bears

Polar bears live near the North Pole. They are strong swimmers and hunt seals and other animals in the sea and on land.

Polar bears have fur and blubber to keep them warm.

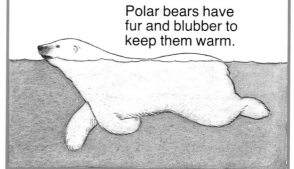

Polar fish

Many polar fish, such as this Antarctic cod, have special chemicals in their blood to stop it from freezing in the chilly water.

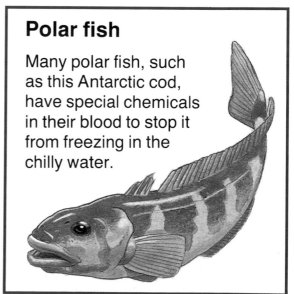

Divers

Divers do all sorts of work under the sea, from mending pipelines to studying the seabed. Most only go down to 50m (160ft). These divers carry a tank of air on their back to breathe from.

This diving suit keeps water out so the diver stays warm and dry.

Coming up

As divers go down, more water presses on them from above. This is called water pressure. Divers must come up very slowly to get used to changes in pressure.

Deep-sea divers

Deep-sea divers work at about 350m (1,000ft). Most breathe a special mix of gases through a pipe. This is sent down to them from a machine called a diving bell.

One of these pipes carries gas. Another pumps hot water around the suit to keep the diver warm.

Hard suits

Some deep-sea divers wear hard suits which protect them from the pressure of the water. They breathe oxygen from tanks inside.

Part of this suit has been cut away to show the diver inside.

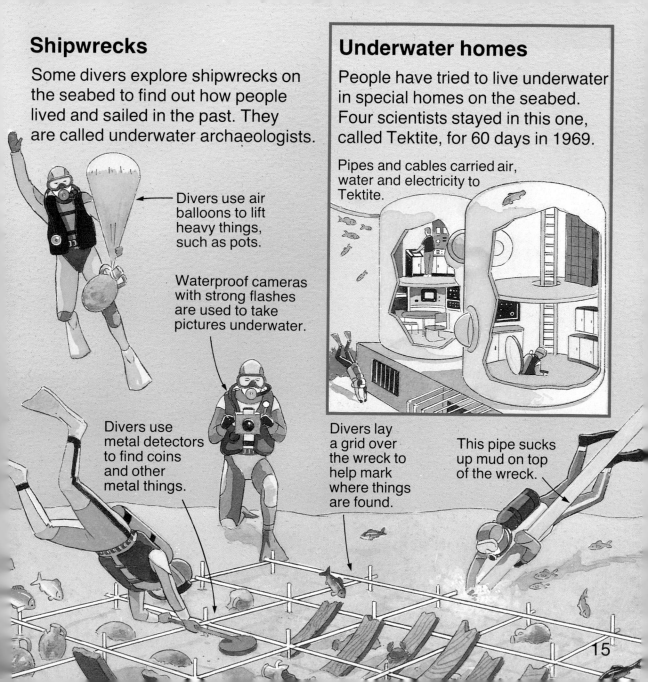

Shipwrecks

Some divers explore shipwrecks on the seabed to find out how people lived and sailed in the past. They are called underwater archaeologists.

Divers use air balloons to lift heavy things, such as pots.

Waterproof cameras with strong flashes are used to take pictures underwater.

Divers use metal detectors to find coins and other metal things.

Underwater homes

People have tried to live underwater in special homes on the seabed. Four scientists stayed in this one, called Tektite, for 60 days in 1969.

Pipes and cables carried air, water and electricity to Tektite.

Divers lay a grid over the wreck to help mark where things are found.

This pipe sucks up mud on top of the wreck.

15

Underwater machines

Underwater machines called submersibles can go even deeper than divers. They have special tools to work underwater. Some submersibles carry people, but most are undersea robots which are controlled from above.

Going down in submersibles

The French submersible, Nautile, can take people down to 6,000m (19,500ft). Its tools are controlled by the crew inside.

Bright lamps light up the dark water.

These arms can pick up things from the seabed.

Interesting things are stored in this tray to look at later.

Cameras take pictures and films underwater.

Giant batteries power Nautile.

The crew breathe air in the cabin. They look out of windows at the front.

Strong walls protect Nautile from the crushing water pressure outside.

Submarines

Submarines are big underwater ships which are used by navies.

Here you can see how tanks inside a submarine help it go up and down.

The tanks are filled with water to let the submarine go down. The water makes it heavy enough to sink.

The tanks are closed to let the submarine stay at the same depth.

The tanks are filled with air to make the submarine light enough to rise. The air pushes the water out.

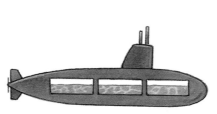

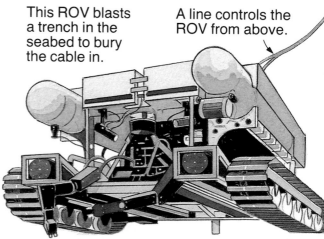

Bathyscaphes

A bathyscaphe is a submersible which explores the deepest oceans. It has a cabin below for the crew.

In 1960, the bathyscaphe Trieste dived almost 11km (7 miles) to the bottom of the Marianas Trench.

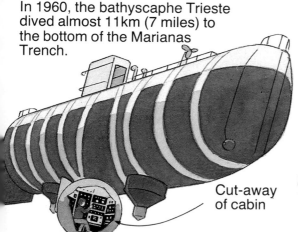

Cut-away of cabin

ROVs

Underwater robots are also known as ROVs. This one is used to mend and bury telephone cables on the seabed.

This ROV blasts a trench in the seabed to bury the cable in.

A line controls the ROV from above.

17

The seabed

The Earth's surface is made up of big pieces called plates. These move slowly on a layer of hot rock called the mantle. This picture shows some of the plates which make up the seabed.

Undersea volcanoes are formed by melted rock, called magma, oozing up through the seabed. The magma cools and hardens into layers of rock. It slowly builds up to form volcanoes.

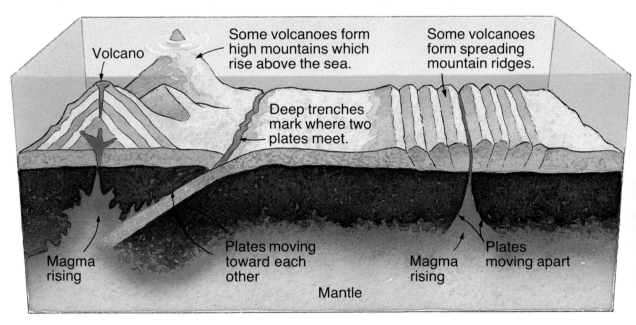

Volcano

Some volcanoes form high mountains which rise above the sea.

Some volcanoes form spreading mountain ridges.

Deep trenches mark where two plates meet.

Magma rising

Plates moving toward each other

Magma rising

Plates moving apart

Mantle

Disappearing seabed

Seabed is always being destroyed. When two plates move toward each other, one plunges underneath. Parts of it melt into magma. Some of this magma may rise to form volcanoes.

New seabed

New seabed is always being made. This happens as two plates move apart. Magma wells up to fill the gap. It forms spreading mountain ridges as it hardens to make new seabed.

Hot springs

Scientists have found hot springs near plate edges. Here, seawater seeps into cracks in the seabed and is heated by hot rocks below. It gushes back up through the seabed in a hot jet.

The hot water collects minerals from rocks below. The minerals make it cloudy.

Cloudy springs are also called smokers.

Minerals in the hot water form a chimney around the spring.

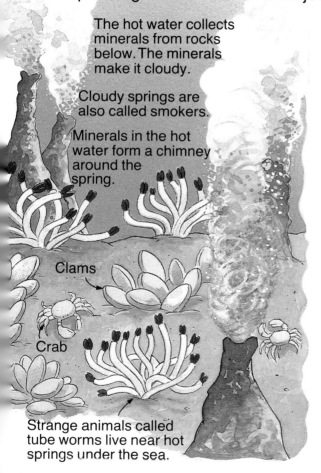

Clams

Crab

Strange animals called tube worms live near hot springs under the sea.

How deep is the sea?

People find out how deep the sea is by timing how long sounds take to echo back from the seabed. They put the different depths together to make a map of the seabed.

A machine called an echo sounder sends out sounds and times their echoes as the ship moves along.

Sound waves

Echoes

Tunnels under the sea

Giant drilling machines can bore huge tunnels through the seabed. The longest railway tunnel under the sea is the Channel Tunnel between England and France.

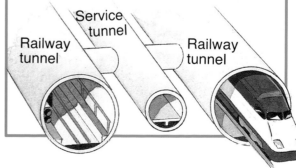

Service tunnel

Railway tunnel

Railway tunnel

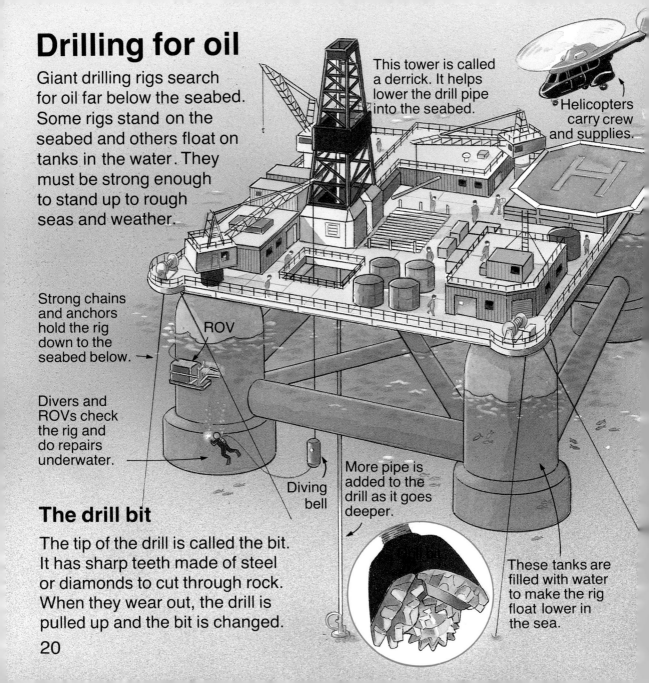

Drilling for oil

Giant drilling rigs search
for oil far below the seabed.
Some rigs stand on the
seabed and others float on
tanks in the water. They
must be strong enough
to stand up to rough
seas and weather.

This tower is called
a derrick. It helps
lower the drill pipe
into the seabed.

Helicopters
carry crew
and supplies.

Strong chains
and anchors
hold the rig
down to the
seabed below.

ROV

Divers and
ROVs check
the rig and
do repairs
underwater.

Diving
bell

More pipe is
added to the
drill as it goes
deeper.

These tanks are
filled with water
to make the rig
float lower in
the sea.

The drill bit

The tip of the drill is called the bit.
It has sharp teeth made of steel
or diamonds to cut through rock.
When they wear out, the drill is
pulled up and the bit is changed.

20

Pumping oil up

Once oil is found, the rig is taken away. A bigger production platform is built to drill more wells and pump oil up.

Carrying oil ashore

Pipelines and tankers carry oil to shore where it is used to make fuel, electricity, plastics, paint and glue.

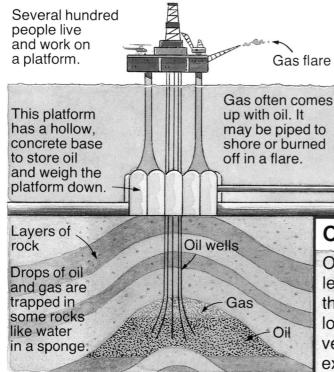

Several hundred people live and work on a platform.

Gas flare

This platform has a hollow, concrete base to store oil and weigh the platform down.

Gas often comes up with oil. It may be piped to shore or burned off in a flare.

The biggest oil tankers can carry 500,000 tonnes (tons) of oil.

Pipelines are coated with concrete to weigh them down. Some are buried, too.

Layers of rock

Oil wells

Drops of oil and gas are trapped in some rocks like water in a sponge.

Gas

Oil

How oil is formed

Oil is formed over millions of years from tiny, dead sea animals. These were buried by mud which hardened into rock. The rock slowly crushed their rotting remains into oil and gas.

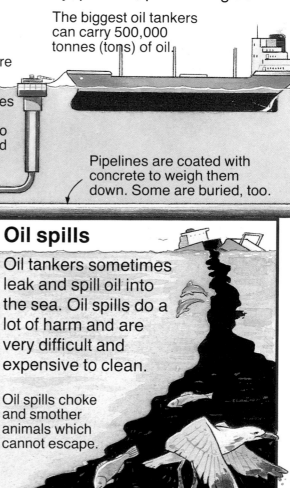

Oil spills

Oil tankers sometimes leak and spill oil into the sea. Oil spills do a lot of harm and are very difficult and expensive to clean.

Oil spills choke and smother animals which cannot escape.

Using the seas

For thousands of years, people have fished the seas for food. Today, modern fishing boats can catch huge amounts of fish at a time in giant nets.

Shellfish

All kinds of shellfish come from the sea. People usually fish for them in shallow seas near the shore.

Oysters   Mussels   Cockles
Crab   Lobster   Prawns

Trawl nets scoop up fish on or near the seabed.

Some fish swim in big groups called shoals. Purse nets are pulled around whole shoals.

Drift nets are stretched out to catch fish. Unfortunately they trap other animals, too.

Some nets have bigger holes. These let baby fish slip out.

Overfishing

Too many fish are caught in some parts of the sea. Baby ones are caught before they can grow and breed. Some countries have agreed to catch fewer fish because of this.

Mining minerals

Useful rocks, minerals and precious stones are also taken from the sea.

Sand and gravel are scooped up from the seabed near coasts and used for building.

In some hot countries, seawater is collected in flat pans near shore. It dries up in the sun, leaving salt behind.

Diamonds are sucked up from the seabed off southwest Africa.

Lumps of a valuable metal called manganese lie on the seabed below the Pacific Ocean. They may one day be mined.

Pearls are found in oysters. They grow around grit inside oysters.

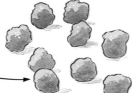

Keeping seas clean

People dump waste in the sea from factories, sewage works and nuclear power stations. Too much waste can pollute the water. Countries need to work together to keep seas clean.

Polluted water can poison fish and other animals.

Lost nets and litter can choke and trap animals.

Index